Win, Win, Win!

The 18 Inclusion-isms You Need
To Become A Disability Confident Employer.

Win, Win, Win!

The 18 Inclusion-isms You Need
To Become A Disability Confident Employer.

By: Tova Sherman,
Award-winning CEO & International Inclusion Expert
Illustrated By: Diverse Nova Scotian Artists

reachAbility Press

Win, Win, Win!

The 18 Inclusion-isms You Need
To Become A Disability Confident Employer

By Tova Sherman

Award-winning CEO & International Inclusion Expert

Win, Win, Win! The 18 Inclusion-isms You Need
To Become A Disability Confident Employer.
Copyright © Tova Sherman 2020

reachAbility Association
3845 Joseph Howe Dr #201, Halifax, NS B3L 4H9 Canada
www.reachAbility.org

Hardcover ISBN: 978-0-9813231-3-8
Paperback ISBN: 978-0-9813231-4-5
eISBN: 978-0-9813231-5-2

This publication is funded in part by the Government of
Canada, Building Communities Through Arts and Heritage -
Local Festivals Component in partnership with the Bluenose
Ability Arts & Film Festival.

Foreword by Aoife MacNamara, President of the
Nova Scotia College of Art and Design March 2020

Title Copyright © Tova Sherman 2019
*Illustrations Copyright © reachAbility 2020
*Jacket Artwork Copyright © reachAbility 2020
First Edition: October 2020
This hardcover edition first published in 2020 by

reachAbility Press

Dedicated to
my mother, Shirley & my daughter, Brachie
the two bookends that hold me together.

Table of Contents

Acknowledgments

Win, Win, Win! The 18 Inclusion-isms You Need to Become A Disability Confident Employer

20 years ago, a gentleman by the name of Dr. Bruce Mills approached me to join him and a small team of stakeholders, dedicated to the inclusion of persons with disabilities, in launching a grassroots agency. The idea was to ensure a voice for people with all types of disabilities and to ensure equal access to services and opportunities. Thanks to his guidance and leadership a small team of dedicated folks have been able to achieve a great deal.

Thank you first and foremost to Jess and the reachAbility team for being willing to take chances in support of the greater good. To the Board of Directors and key stakeholders, your confidence in our work has kept us going more than you know.

To the hundreds of organizations, and thousands of clients who have looked to reachAbility Association for leadership and support in inclusion over the past 20 years—we welcome you to continue working side by side with us—toward a fair and equitable community.

I also wish to acknowledge my siblings; Beila, Garry, Dawn and Miryawm who have been so kind to their little sister despite some of her less flattering ADHD-SD behaviours.

Finally; to Jœy, a big thank you for all your efforts in keeping the content, and me, in-line.

Foreword

Win, Win, Win. recognizes that creativity and culture play a central role in supporting local economies and talent, health and wellbeing. It illustrates how together in all our diversity we—children, youth, adults and seniors—have been flourishing in our creativity, and that we have been strengthened in our work by partnerships with business, communities and local and national government. Working together we are opening up new avenues of expression and ways of working in art and culture. Together our diverse and inclusive perspective is helping change the way we think about who museums, libraries and arts organizations are for, and, in so doing we are improving the lives of people everywhere.

Understanding of the role of culture in building and sustaining communities is at the heart of the work included in *Win, Win, Win.* The artists help us focus on what matters to all of us, and why. The artists included here benefit from being part of a wider cultural community at a point when Canada is redefining our internal relationships and our relationships with the world. Canada's diverse cultural perspectives and culture are a national asset and gives us a unique international advantage, encouraging us to converse and collaborate freely across generations, geographies and abilities.

The work included here illustrates some of the significant differences in what art and culture mean to different people, in different places and from across all stages of life. The diversity in the work here challenges the idea that art is only associated with a particular style of visual arts, or with what are often called 'high art' forms. Instead, what the art in *Win, Win, Win!* shows is that there are many ways to make art and have an active cultural life, and that people of all ages, abilities and backgrounds value the opportunity to have a active cultural life.

The importance of art and culture to all communities is not reflected in the opportunities people have to access art, as makers, audiences or critics. There are still widespread socio-economic, geographic and ability variances in who gets to engage in art and publicly funded culture here in Canada. The opportunities for children, youth and adults to experience creativity and culture inside and outside school are not equal. There remains a persistent and widespread lack of diversity across the creative industries and in publicly funded cultural organizations. Organizations like reachAbility are heightening awareness of the issue is greater, and helping to change who gets to make culture and creativity part of our lives.

Looking at the work here, it's easy believe that the creativity and culture are deeply connected, but different. Creativity is the process by which, either individually or with others, we make something new: a work of art, or a reimagining of an existing work. Everyone needs to have more opportunities for both: to be creative, and to experience high-quality culture. Having the time and tools to develop personal creative potential can be profoundly fulfilling, while engaging in culture is helps inspire our imaginations. Taken together, they can help us make sense of ourselves and of each other in all our diversity: they provoke and uplift us; they unite communities; and they bring us joy. If access to either creativity or culture is limited by where people come from, what abilities they have, or what they do, the whole of society loses out.

- Aoife MacNamara, President NSCAD
(Nova Scotia College of Art & Design) 2020

Introduction

Thank you for taking your first step towards becoming a disability confident employer. Whether you have experience in inclusive hiring or are just getting started, this book is an important amalgamation of over 20 years of trial and error resulting in best practices. In fact, I often say we must do better than best practices—by developing NEXT practices. As an unabashed ADHD-influenced risk-taker I am committed to doing more than just walking the path – I'm blazing the trail.

Whether you've purchased this book for yourself, or it was gifted to you, I guarantee that this brief and thought-provoking book will teach you something about the ease of creating an inclusive workplace culture that you didn't know before.

These 18 tried and true Inclusion-isms; with each "ism" providing a workplace definition, application and artist interpretation are laid out for quick reference and easy to share. The goal is for you to not only read this but use the tools (especially the "In Practice" sections) within your office right now. The ability for you to communicate what you want was just made easier by the 18 Inclusion-isms covered.

I hope you enjoy this book. It is the perfect guide to getting started or upgrading your goals for an inclusive workplace—now that is a win, win, win!

Win, Win, Win!

When the renowned business author, Steven Covey (*The 7 Habits of Highly Effective People*) introduced the idea of win, win in 1989, he invited both the car salesman and the car buyer to each have a win, creating a mutually beneficial situation.

His message was; instead of someone having to lose in the deal—both can win if the car salesman makes money on the vehicle and the buyer gets a reasonably good deal on their new car. The result, the buyer will likely return; and hopefully, tell others about how fairly they were treated etc. That is the concept behind win, win.

I have taken that idea to the next level; which is where win, win, win originated.

In a workplace, the third win can be established through the inclusion of diverse job seekers in your hiring pool and the overflowing benefit it has on the overall community.

So when I say win, win, win I am referring to the employer, the consumer and the diverse workforce that provides your workplace with a fresh perspective and demonstrates a truly creative approach to how things can get done. Consider three wins in your next hiring decision.

In Practice: Identify in your workplace an existing win, win, win scenario. If there is none; now is the time to instill the message with your entire hiring team; so that moving forward the search for three wins is a given.

Artist:
Geoffrey Cwiklewich

GAGNER
ВИГРАТИ
VOITTAA
LANAKILA
GANAR
ZMAGA
VINCERE
KUSHINDA
GANHAR
NIKH
ZDOBYĆ
WIN

Diversity Without Inclusion is Like a House Without a Foundation

The truth is you may be great at finding and hiring all kinds of folks from various backgrounds including; newcomers, visible minorities and persons with disabilities, etc. (aka the House) - which translates into a diverse workforce. Where employers often struggle is on the inclusion piece (aka the foundation).

You may have the most diverse workforce but if leaders are not knowledgeable on what makes an inclusive workplace—where everyone is welcomed and accommodated in order to equalize the playing field—then you have built a house without any foundation.

Houses lacking foundations tend to collapse.

So remember there are two parts to including diverse populations in your workplace: ensuring your team is aware of your desire to be both diverse and inclusive and providing them the tools to succeed in doing so.

In Practice: How often do you provide your team (from the top down & the bottom up) access to learning around diversity & inclusion?

If your answer is rarely or never: it is time to change that. How? Agencies, like reachAbility, provide new knowledge, as it relates to inclusion, in communities all across Canada. Reach out to one near year today!

Artist:
Trudy Fong

There are Two Ways to Ensure Inclusion: Education & Osmosis

In my travels as an accessibility, diversity and inclusion trainer I am always able to spot individuals who have worked with persons living with all types of disabilities, simply by how they respond to my tips on inclusion. For instance: if I am discussing the ease of accommodating someone who uses a wheelchair and see a participant in the classroom nodding their head up and down enthusiastically, I can almost promise you that person has worked with/knows well a person who uses a wheelchair. The head nod reflects their participation and comfort with the suggested accommodations. That's what I call osmosis: having worked alongside a person with disability is one of two key ways to remove stigma from your workplace and create a truly inclusive culture.

The other way is unlikely news to anyone—which makes it all the more surprising that it is so rarely found—I am referring to the importance of education around disability for your entire team. Having developed and disseminated all levels of diversity and inclusion training I can assure you people are surprised by what they discover about inclusion—most of them for the very first time.

In Practice: Have you ever provided your management team actual information on your commitment to inclusion? The newly minted ACA: Accessible Canada Act (2019) makes now the perfect time to ensure you are compliant with the current accessibility standards. Start by reaching out to the experts (www.reachAbility.org)

Artist:
Eleanor Hannon

The Fish Stinks From the Head

Being from the East Coast it is natural for me to think in terms of, well, fish. But as a CEO I take the responsibility of being in charge very seriously. In the workplace; my messaging is key to success.

The fact is a leader's tone, style and messaging matters. If inclusion is important to you then it must be made clear through more than just words and policy shifts—but with a clear plan in place that shows the entire team you are committed to a diverse, inclusive workplace.

In the United States the ADA (Americans with Disabilities Act) and in Canada The ACA (Accessible Canada Act) represent the best in workplace standards. Step 1 is to take a look and ensure you are compliant.

There may be very capable members of the team who want to ensure a welcoming workplace—and they are to be rewarded for their commitment. But it will take clear messaging from the top if diversity is to be seen as part of everyone's core responsibilities—rather than just more work for your HR team.

In Practice: Take a close look at your most recent job ad(s) and ask yourself; when is the last time the verbiage was changed and does it reflect your inclusive hiring strategy?

Artist:
Lee Cripps

Stigma's Power is in Silence

In other words; stigma of persons living with disabilities in the workplace and beyond continues because we do not talk about it. People often choose not to discuss what they don't understand and that is why myths about disability continue to persist.

Studies across North America continue to report employees with disabilities have fewer sick days and higher loyalty, thus staying longer, so why the concerns?

Education of your existing team is crucial to building the foundation required to ensure a healthy, happy workplace filled with diverse people. Silence can no longer be an option in the workplace; and leaders must replace it with honest conversation.

In Practice: Reflection

Where did you first learn about disability (for example; schoolyard, TV, news program, etc.)?

How was the source of your knowledge of persons with disabilities defined by that experience?

Expand on these questions by posing them to your team (based on your comfort level).

Artist:
Lindsey Reid

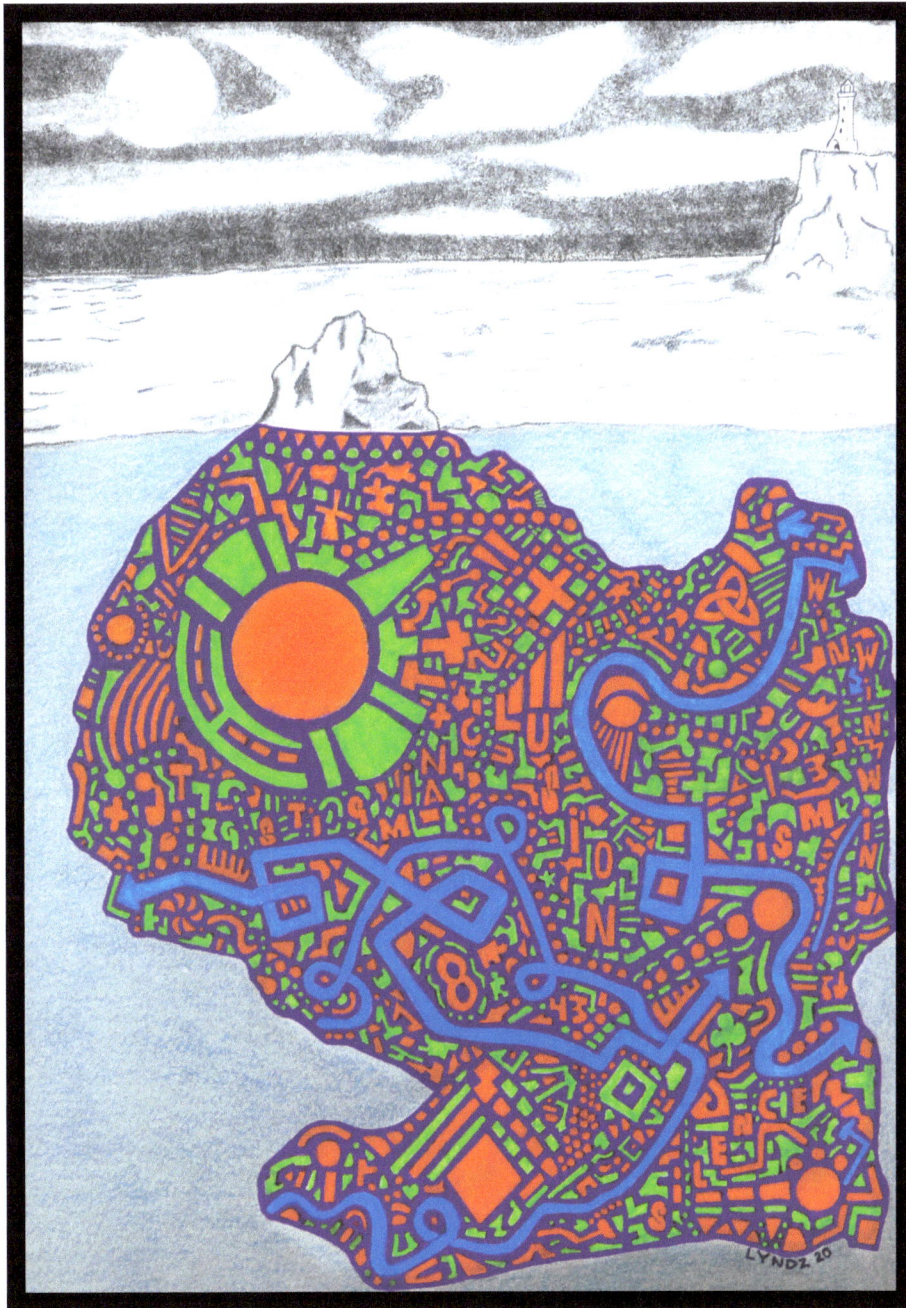

Everyone has Had, has or Will Have a Disability

We need to reflect on not just what disability really means but also the fact that at some point in our lives we will all experience the additional challenges living with disability can present.

Whether episodic (i.e. a broken leg from skiing that will return to normal), developmental (i.e. born on the ADHD Spectrum) or acquired (i.e. brain injury from a car accident) we must remember stigmatizing persons with disabilities is stigmatizing you and everyone you care about.

One need not think very hard to bring to mind a person they care a great deal about living with disability right now.

After all, everyone has had, has or will have a disability, so who are we stigmatizing?

In Practice: There are 5 categories of disability; physical, mental, cognitive, sensory and invisible. Are you aware of some of the types of disabilities that fall under each?

If not, now is a great time to look it up—and feel free to share your wealth of knowledge on the matter. After all, knowledge is power!

Artist:
Susan MacLeod

We've been married 75 years.
Met in Grade 3 at the Chebucto School.
Mom and Dad got along just fine too.
He always gave into me. →
We always had dogs.
Four boys.
SUSAN MACLEOD 2017

People Don't Come with Instructions

Have you ever tried to assemble furniture from one of those "it's so easy to put together you won't believe it" places? If you have then you know a bookshelf is assembled in the exact same manner no matter what language you speak or where you live. Those step by step drawings never alter.

People, on the other hand are unique beings; each with our own needs and wants. In the case of those of us who live with disabilities—of which I am one—you can not presume to know me just because you perhaps know someone else with the same diagnosis. I am not "ADHD Tova" but rather Tova who lives with a disability. The disability does not define me—but it can be a pain in the ass (as my 89 year old mother likes to remind me).

It comes down to not jumping to conclusions.

In Practice: The ability to listen to what staff require to be successful is an important aspect of management that many overlook. If that is not yet built into your orientation process, now is the time to do so. Ensure the entire team is aware of how important inclusive onboarding (and inclusion of all staff) is to you.

Artist:
Eleanor Hannon

Dignity: Plain & Simple

Immediately after my mother lost her voice box to cancer I would frequently try to read her lips, especially when she was too tired to write out what she wanted to say. Today, she communicates very well with a wonderful assistive device known as a Cervox.

Previous to the arrival of the Cervox and clearly frustrated by my weak attempts to "assume what she meant", my mother one day put her tiny hand in my face to signal that I should stop talking and with the other, she handed me a note. This is what it said:

I know you love me but when you try to guess what I am saying and do not show the patience to really understand me - you are removing my basic dignity. Why? Because you are saying it is not important enough for you to take the time to truly comprehend me; that it is easier to pretend you get it. And that my dear daughter is robbing me of my dignity: plain & simple.

In Practice: Never pretend to understand someone if you really don't. Even if it is slightly uncomfortable to ask them to repeat themselves—they will appreciate your effort.

Artist:
Kathy Kaulbach

Just Because You Can't See it Doesn't Mean it isn't There

On the surface this may seem counterintuitive. For people with invisible disabilities often co-workers will think they are faking an impairment or simply "being lazy" and this causes issues at work.

Frank is a burly guy, about 6'2". Frank was in a serious car accident and broke his collarbone. After years of rehab he returns to work. He has told his employer about his physical limitations and although we can not see it (invisible disability) we know it is going to affect his ability to help out with any lifting/moving around the office. When co-workers see a big burly guy shying away from helping the team move things; people forget why and start to judge—even thinking less of him despite his excellent work ethic.

We must resist the instinct to trust only our eyes and get to know who our team is and their individual strengths and challenges.

In Practice: Ensure the entire team knows you are committed to accommodate and support changes in staff capacity as part of your overall inclusion strategy.

Artist:
Dorothyanne Brown

Screen in, Not out

Anyone who has read a book or attended a class, in the field of Human Resources (HR), knows the term Screen Out. The goal of this popular practice is to trim down the number of resumes requiring a closer look. The more resumes you screen out—for reasons ranging from gaps in education, timeline or years on the job—the better.

My experience has proven over and over again that by screening in you may find some dedicated, loyal team members who have incredible character and skills to make a great match with you and your workplace culture.

To be clear, I am not suggesting a surgeon doesn't need a medical degree. I am suggesting that just because there is a gap in a resume doesn't mean the applicant is not right for the job. What if the reason for that year off was their choice to take care of a parent in their last year of life? Behavior like that screams loyal, dedicated, committed - now that is an employee I could get behind; how about you?

In Practice: Ensure you share your philosophy of screening in with all members of your hiring and management team(s). The last thing you want is to miss out on a great employee because of outdated practices.

Artist:
Nigel Beck

Right Person, Right Job

In more than two decades of consulting on inclusion in the workplace, people are often surprised to learn that my agency has rarely applied a wage subsidy when placing someone in employment. The reason is simple; I believe if it is not the right person for the job, all the subsidy in the world won't help. Conversely; if they are right for the job then subsidy should not be necessary.

As an employer looking to engage diverse populations you already understand the importance of being open to doing the job in different ways—just as long as it gets done—and done well.

Right Person, Right Job is a battle-cry that invites employers to embrace different ways of getting the job done; to imagine diverse jobseekers accomplishing great things—because this is the right job for them.

In Practice: Look at the job description of the last position you hired for (or perhaps one needing to be filled). Now ask yourself if any of the items listed assume how to do something vs what needs to be accomplished. The difference may seem subtle at first but it really matters to the job seeker, and will ensure more diverse job applicants apply.

Artist:
Meghan Macdonald

Revise, Revisit, Reassess

With all new employees there is a period involving accommodation. In the case of some it may be as simple as acclimatizing to the new environment. For others it may require an accommodation relating to their disability. Remember accommodation is about equalizing the playing field for all—nothing "special" about it.

In the case of accommodation I always say:

Revise; consult with employee and make changes based on dialogue—after all they know more about how they get things done than you do.

Revisit; Accommodation is an ongoing reality. If you have an employee returning after being off, their progress may improve over time. That is why it is so important to revisit the original accommodation.

Reassess; That's right, check-ins are not only a good idea but ensure an equalized playing field for all involved.

In Practice: If you have any accommodation in place; from revised hours to workspace setup, now is the time to check in and ask how it is going and what needs to be revised.

Artist:
Heidi Hallett

Pitch, Don't Bitch

Equalizing the playing field also means expecting a high level of excellence for and from the entire team. As a leader, I expect my entire team to be problem-solvers; something persons with disabilities excel at due to the constant problem-solving required when you live in a world not built for you.

When an employee comes into my office with a problem I always ask them what solutions they have tried/come up with. The bitch is the issue—but it is the pitch I am interested in cultivating. By giving everyone permission to share their ideas for addressing a given challenge you are building a solutions-based team. Now that is a win, win, win.

Pitch, Don't Bitch is a request to staff to take a moment and consider how they might solve the issue before moving it up the ladder.

In Practice: This is an easy one. Challenge the next person who brings you an issue to share their ideas for solving it. They will feel engaged and hopefully you may agree and provide them approval to proceed.

Artist:
Lee Cripps

Even When Architectural Barriers are Removed, Attitudinal ones still Remain

Anytime you walk into a newer hotel the doors will sleekly open and the entrance has a easy to manage surface. I imagine people with luggage, families with kids in strollers appreciating the ease of access to the front desk. This hotel is welcoming to persons with disabilities; at least for people with physical disabilities; and that is great news because we want a welcoming space that can be accessed by anyone using a wheelchair or other assistive device for physical reasons.

The fact is, it may not be a very welcoming place for people with other types of disabilities, and without proper training the staff are unlikely to understand how to equalize the playing field for any guest, no matter what their accommodation need might be.

Attitudinal barriers are where stigma lives, created by the perpetuation of myths as they relate to people with disabilities.

So remember just because there is a ramp at the door does not mean the space is inclusive of persons with disabilities; because disability is much more than just physical. It is the attitudinal barriers that must be addressed first and foremost.

In Practice: Identify an accommodation in your workplace that is not physical in nature. If you can not find one consider adding one. For accommodation ideas check out: www.reachAbility.org

Artist:
Nigel Beck

Call to remove barriers

I Want to Make You Bolder not Better

On its surface this Inclusion-ism can seem harsh if misunderstood.

I am your boss; not your therapist, not your friend, and not your confidant. I cannot make you feel better but I can support you in becoming a bold, inclusive voice in our workplace.

As a Leader committed to inclusion of persons with disabilities in mainstream workplaces across North America, my goal is to develop bold leaders who are willing to challenge themselves and those around them - in support of inclusion. We all win when we can empower the team from the top down to creatively approach challenges and not be afraid to share their ideas.

The ability to empower your team is how to develop resilient leaders of the future.

In Practice: Ensure your team is clear on how leadership can support them in being more successful at work. Lead that discussion when possible – to show your personal commitment to strengthening dialogue.

Artist:
Tara Grude

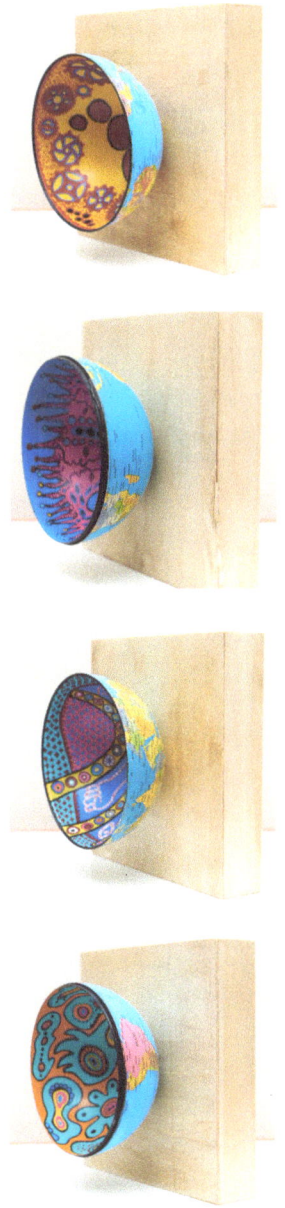

Stay Curious

When I speak of being truly curious I don't mean the 'what the heck is wrong with you' kind of curious. Authentic curiosity is just another term for genuine engagement. I am always interested in why a member of my team is doing/saying something that I find, well, curious. The jump to assuming we know what is happening can be a seductive trap. After all we have seen it all before, right?

Truth is, staying curious means you are open to various problem-solving viewpoints. It shows the entire team that as a leader you are curious enough to want to encourage diverse perspectives and approaches to achieving success. The ability to let someone be heard cannot be understated.

In Practice: Encourage your management team to answer questions such as: why are we doing this activity and what do we expect to happen as a result? It is this kind of curiosity that encourages highly successful, innovative thinking. Success can be one question away.

Artist:
Kirsten Carter

Inclusion is Different, not Difficult

When it comes to engaging diverse populations in the workplace the myth is; it is a hard thing to do. That can not be further from the truth. Most disability-related workplace accommodations are affordable and the majority of people with higher needs bring their own accommodation.

The idea that employing a person with disability creates too many challenges is outdated and unproven. The sooner leadership embraces the ease of accommodation and the value of inclusion, the sooner you will be blazing the trail for others to follow.

Although 90% of companies claim to prioritize diversity, only 4% consider disability, according to a report from *The Harvard Business Review*.

We can all do better and the entire workplace benefits when we do.   Our workforce should represent our diverse community and there are simple steps we can all take to make it possible.

In Practice: If you agree with this statement; say so. Add it to key messaging for all team members.

Artist:
Trudy Fong

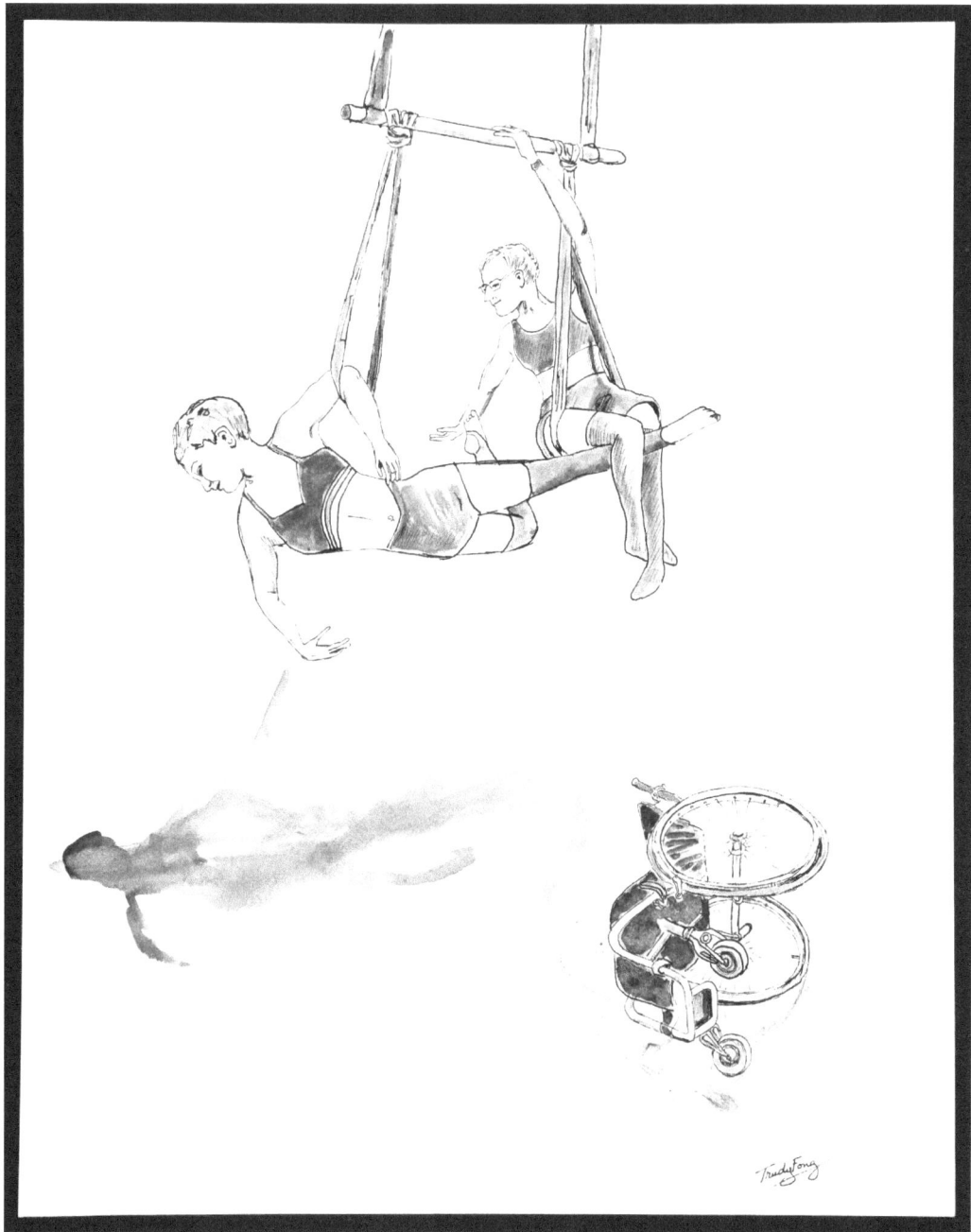

I Make a Difference because I Can

If there is one Inclusion-ism that defines my personal beliefs it is this one.

Many years ago I came across a quote from an American author who lived in the 19th century, Edward Everett Hale. He wrote: "I am only one, but I am one. I can't do everything, but I can do something. The something I ought to do, I can do. And by the grace of God, I will."

As a leader who has definite limitations, this quote really spoke to me. It reminded me that although there is plenty I cannot do, there is plenty I can do—and I must never let what I cannot do stop me from doing all I can. Confused yet?

As leaders we have responsibility to get the best out of our team; and if we apply all that we do know about how to get things done—amazing things can happen.

In Practice: Apply all 18 Inclusion-isms and watch your entire team, from the bottom up, feel empowered and engaged like never before.

Artist:
Tyler Hayden

Artist Index

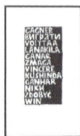

1. Win, Win, Win!
About the Artist: Geoffrey Cwiklewich is a designer and printer who lives in Halifax, NS. His current work draws inspiration from words and language and how the way they are used affects the way we perceive people and the environment around us.

About the Art: This piece shows the word 'win' in twelve different languages. "Win, Win, Win reminds me of the many possible benefits we can get from connecting with people with different experiences from our own."

2. Diversity Without Inclusion is Like a House Without a Foundation
About the Artist: Trudy Fong worked for many years as a journalist and author before embracing her inner artist. She is particularly clumsy and following several severe falls, she had a complete hip replacement. Relearning how to walk was her wake-up call. When she's not creating art or writing, she cares for several relatives with health challenges. Trudy lives in Dartmouth, Nova Scotia.

About the Art: A house without a foundation is as useful as coffee without a cup. "The rainbow painting was inspired by my experience as a mother of LGBTQ+ kids and an understanding of the challenges they face regarding acceptance."

3. There are Two Ways to Ensure Inclusion: Education & Osmosis
About the Artist: Eleanor Hannon is a Halifax-based illustrator and recent fine arts graduate of NSCAD University. She is passionate about art, accessibility, and how the two intersect.

About the Art: "When I think about 'education and osmosis', I picture how much we learn, implicitly and explicitly, when we talk to each other."

4. The Fish Stinks From the Head
About the Artist: Lee Cripps is a Dartmouth-born multidisciplinary artist, curator, mother, and spiritualist. She is prone to anxiety-wrapped-neuroses, a lovely first course to stress-induced panic attacks, and finding four-leaf-clovers. "Daydreaming is an art and gives me time to breathe".

About the Art: "My painting for the fish stinks from the head, was an examination of the many ways we take on leadership roles in our lives. Through family, friendships, work, and community roles, we often find ourselves leading in small and big ways. These roles have the potential to become more like relationships and conversations and can immensely feed the souls of all involved with tremendous joy and fulfillment."

5. Stigma's Power is in Silence
About the Artist: Lindsey Reid uses art to express her internal experience as a way of sharing her perspectives with others. As a person with a traumatic brain injury, her art expresses her experience of having an invisible disability.

About the Art: "I experience the stigma that comes from people not recognizing that I have a disability because I'm not wearing a cast or have a visible difference. But they do notice that I'm different and they judge me quietly. They see the tip of my iceberg, but my art shows them the invisible world under my surface."

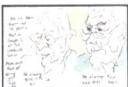

6. Everyone Has Had, Has, or Will Have a Disability
About the Artist: Susan MacLeod began drawing older adults while shepherding her mother through nine years of long-term care. She is currently writing a humorous graphic memoir about the many communication failures that plagued them both throughout that underground and unseen experience.

About the Art: "I began drawing my mother's fellow nursing home residents to help cope with the unease I felt around them. I quickly learned that they are no different than any other adult, though often a great deal more fun and loads more interesting. The very old, like everyone, yearn to be seen, heard, and valued. Drawing them was a way to do just that."

7. People Don't Come with Instructions
About the Artist: Eleanor Hannon is a Halifax-based illustrator and recent fine arts graduate of NSCAD University. She is passionate about art, accessibility, and how the two intersect.

About the Art: This is a self-portrait illustrating accommodations that I may need in relation to my own disability. Looking at the figure on the left you may have no idea what they need until you relate to them on an individual level.

8. Dignity: Plain and Simple
About the Artist: Kathy Kaulbach is a Nova Scotia designer/illustrator. The goal of her work is to present information visually to create content that fosters understanding. This project unveils disabilities and calls for understanding. Kathy dedicates this work to her friends, loved ones, and all those who balance daily on an edge.

About the Art: "We all know people who struggle with disabilities whether they are verbal, like this image, or in another form. To show our respect and love, please stop and listen to their story."

9. Just Because You Can't See it Dœsn't Mean it isn't There
About the Artist: Dorothyanne Brown is a former health care manager and nurse who had to leave work due to the cognitive effects of Multiple Sclerosis. She is a fibre artist, embroiderer, and freelance writer.

About the Art: "Because my MS has caused mostly cognitive and mood changes, I often appear fine. This piece is meant to illustrate the hidden, but still present, brain changes in people who, like me, have brain damage; those with PTSD, depression, MS, or other brain injury."

10. Screen in, Not out
About the Artist: Nigel Beck is a Yorkshire native and Royal Airforce veteran of 23 years. Since moving to Nova Scotia in 2010, he has become a photographer and mental health advocate.

About the Art: Think of the TV as Recruitment/ Human Resources personnel. The larger arrow is the screening out, but on reflection, and with the reflection on the TV itself, it shows how very little gets accepted.

11.Right Person, Right Job

About the Artist: Meghan Macdonald is a textile artist and designer living in Halifax, Nova Scotia. Her creative practice includes making versions of everyday objects in alternative materials.

About the Art: This pocket knife is made of many layers of thread; stitches stitched upon stitches to form a textile. I like how this soft object doesn't do the same job that its steel counterpart does. It functions in its own way, providing a different kind of enjoyment for the viewer.

12. Revise, Revisit, Reassess

About the Artist: Heidi Hallett is a mixed media artist with a passion for art journaling. Having a daily art practice is key to Heidi's wellbeing and management of illness and anxiety. As someone with an invisible illness, Heidi uses her art as a form of self expression and loves teaching others how they can process complex emotions and life challenges through art.

About the Art: The phrase, "Revisit, Reassess, Revise" reminds me of how I approach my art. Being a mixed media artist who works primarily with found objects and upcycled materials, my process is all about revisiting, reassessing, and revising. I revisit materials and reassess how they may be used in different ways and I am constantly revising my art through the use of layers and textures. In terms of the workplace, I have a good deal of personal experience with the need for policies and practices to be followed up on and revisited, reassessed, and revised regularly to ensure they are working. Sadly, in my experience, this is often overlooked.

13. Pitch Don't Bitch

About the Artist: Lee Cripps is a Dartmouth-born multidisciplinary artist, curator, mother, and spiritualist. She is prone to anxiety-wrapped-neuroses, a lovely first course to stress-induced panic attacks, and finding four-leaf-clovers. "Daydreaming is an art and gives me time to breathe".

About the Art: Pitch, don't bitch! Had me considering the many ways I can fall prey to my internal 'Negative Nelly' and how I try (and sometimes, actually succeed!) in shedding a positive light on what may seem like an impossibly challenging situation."

14. Even When Architectural Barriers are Removed, Attitudinal ones still Remain

About the Artist: Nigel Beck is a Yorkshire native and Royal Airforce veteran of 23 years. Since moving to Nova Scotia in 2010, he has become a photographer and mental health advocate.

About the Art: "Nowadays, there are those that don't know how to operate this kind of phone. That embarrassment and feeling of isolation from not knowing how it works, easily translates to those with cognitive and/or mental disabilities. Over time, you learn how to use the phone, you make the call, and the physical barrier is removed. But the light is fading, you can't read the sign, you don't know where you're heading - but you must not stop!!! For every fearful step forward is one more closer to inclusion."

15. I Want to Make You Bolder not Better

About the Artist: Tara Grude is an interdisciplinary artist living in Dartmouth, Nova Scotia. She is passionate about art as a tool for people to connect with both themselves and each other and the difference this can make at an individual or community level.

About the Art: This piece directly references the artwork of Yayoi Kusama, who lives by choice in a mental hospital, and creates artwork that immerses viewers in her intriguing worlds. While we may not be able to cure disability, we can engage those who live with it, empowering and enabling all people to participate and contribute valuable perspectives that enhance the worlds we live and work in.

16. Stay Curious

About the Artist: Kirsten Carter is a Nova Scotia artist who lives with an invisible disability. She started drawing as a way of coping with school and to improve her memory.

About the Art: "I believe animals and young children are the pinnacle of curiosity. When we are young, we are always asking questions and open to learning. Thinking of the quote "Stay Curious", I thought of children looking up at what is a young dragon in curiosity rather than disregarding it as another kite. The mythical critter, curiously trying to make friends with a dragon kite it thinks is another dragon, represents how, even as we grow, we should never stop being curious and continue to learn or we might miss something or fail to connect with those around us."

17. Inclusion is Different, not Difficult

About the Artist: Trudy Fong worked for many years as a journalist and author before embracing her inner artist. She is particularly clumsy and following several severe falls, she had a complete hip replacement. Relearning how to walk was her wake-up call. When she's not creating art or writing, she cares for several relatives with health challenges. Trudy lives in Dartmouth, Nova Scotia.

About the Art: "When I heard this quote, I thought of the circus performer April Hubbard. I am personally very inspired by her determination to do something scary and demanding, knowing that she has pushed way beyond. I think it's important for people to see people with disabilities not just for their challenges but also for the determination that they have developed to do the unusual and brave things that many able-bodied people are too afraid to try. We need to look at the capabilities of people who have learned to put themselves out there despite the challenges."

18. I Make a Difference Because I Can

About the Artist: Tyler Hayden is a motivational speaker and author from Lunenburg, Nova Scotia. His busy mind and hands are a gift delivered from ADHD. When he was out of work, he discovered folk art to keep them busy.

About the Art: Abilities of super proportions are often incognito. As a person with ADHD, my squirrel is the source of my superpowers.

About the Author

Tova's overall vision is that of an equalized playing field. Where those with physical, cognitive, sensory, and mental disabilities can all get the accommodations they require. "Not only the ramp for someone in a wheelchair but also adjust for someone with autism." Diversity is crucial but without inclusivity, it is limited in its impact; architectural change is helpful but without attitudinal change it is futile. "It is not about special treatment; it is about dignity, plain and simple."

As a trailblazer in inclusion and accessibility, Tova saw a gap in the arts community and co-founded the Bluenose Ability Arts and Film Festival (BAAFF) in 2015. BAAFF is a festival dedicated to providing the disability arts community a clear voice. While the festival continues as an annual event celebrating and embracing the talent within the disability arts community, BAAFF has grown to be much more.

From her TED Talk to her tv show, Tova is most recognized for her unique style, great sense of humour and deeply passionate commitment to the inclusion of all our citizens. Her understanding of business, the law and the challenges of inclusion make her a perfect resource in today's swiftly changing employment landscape.

The youngest of five children, Tova has been around disability her entire life. Her own challenges, living on the ADHD Spectrum, inform her empathy and commitment to equalizing the playing field.

In addition to her inclusion efforts Tova most enjoys spending time with her daughter, Brachie, son-in-law Ari and 3 grandsons; Nadav, Gilad & Lev.

To reach out to Tova to speak at your event e-mail her at tova@reachAbility.org

How to order the book

If you or someone you know wishes to order this book directly from the source just:

email: info@reachAbility.org
Call: 902.429-5878
Fax: 902.429.5858

NGO, Library & Post-Secondary discounts available.

www.ingramcontent.com/pod-product-compliance
Lightning Source LLC
Chambersburg PA
CBHW050911210326
41597CB00002B/93